The World On My Plate

ROBIN DAUMIT

www.whiskanddine.com

Cover by Ana Fallon Photography

© 2019 Robin Daumit

ISBN: 978-1-54396-494-3

TABLE OF CONTENTS

THERE'S NO PLACE LIKE HOME.

No one knows me better or forgives my stumbling's through life more than my sisters. Each one of us collectively reflects the most beautiful characteristics of our mom. Through poverty and wealth, tragedy and exuberance, her durability always shone through in a consistent magical way, 'light the stove and let's cook something'!

Cooking made everything smile. Cooking brought laughter to the table, new faces through our front door and a warmth not only to our tummies, but to our hearts as well. This is a feeling shared with my sisters, our children, and now our grandchildren. My deepest thanks will always reside first with my mom, and the magnificent family she created.

My children. You are, and always have been, the love that inspires my every breath.

A smile of thanks also to my hubby who never says 'no' to any of my wild ideas. It's either because he's just as kooky as me, or he knows I have a Genie lamp in my back pocket!

THANKS…

INTRODUCTION

Cooking, for me, is more than food. It's a celebration of people, stories, laughter, flavors, and techniques from a collage of life's excursions.

Before I ever took my first trip, multi-ethnic foods were already being prepared in my mother's kitchen. An American born Syrian, she brought a rainbow of foods to our table as she shared her kitchen with her many girlfriends of various ethnic heritages.

Back in those days, America in the early 50's, women found comfort in sharing friendships with other women of similar backgrounds. Many aromas emitted from our home; Middle Eastern, Greek, Italian, Russian, Armenian, and on the rare occasion, a relative or two from my father's Scandinavian clan.

Once a month, my parents would load my sisters and I into our baby blue Chevy Bel Air, and head to the heart of DC to the Middle Eastern Market for the most sought-after groceries our kitchen stored, which were never available at the local grocery store. Rich sheep milk cheeses from Armenia and Syria, olives that made your mouth water as their briny scent rose from the oily wood barrels on the floor, massive baskets of freshly baked breads of all sizes and shapes, and then there were rows upon rows of well stocked dry goods with labels I couldn't read, but I knew they gave our food more flavor than any other food I had eaten, anywhere!

The pressed sheets of apricots from Lebanon were always the first package I reached for to place in my mother's cart. The soft swishing sound of bulgur wheat being scooped into a paper bag, as a gentle cloud of grain dust rose from the barrel, made my eyes glisten with expectancy as I could already imagine the salads and ground meat dishes we would make with the wheat. Spices unheard of in American food, were always my favorite to explore. Honey straight from bee farms of Morocco and Greece, molasses and syrups made from fruits rarely sold in America, and the dates, oh, the sweet, sweet dates still drying in a cluster on the strand.

Yes, the laughter, the excitement, the dance of anticipation that wove throughout the wooden barrels of faraway foods, to the rhythm of music never heard on the radio, on a wide planked floor that creaked like the sounds of home. A buzz of languages I didn't understand, and yet I imagined they were stories of memories to cherish a lifetime. Here, is where my first love affair with ethnic cuisines tantalized me as a child.

As a grown woman, there are few things I can't cook. My taste buds were first awakened as a child, and throughout my life, my travels and intimate encounters simply built on a tongue that was already passionate and well-formed for flavor.

I'm afraid it may take more than one cookbook to share all the recipes rising up from my life's experience, like the smoke from a Genie bottle, but I will do my best to intrigue you with this one. And what better place to start, than with Small-Plates!

MEZE
TAPAS
APPETIZER
IZAKAYA
MEZETHAKIA
ANTIPASTO
HORS D' OEUVRE
DIM SUM
SMALL PLATES

WHY DO WE NEED ANYTHING ELSE!

I want it all, when I am dining, and the main course is not necessarily the star of the meal. I'm the sort of person that orders three or four appetizers at a restaurant, in preference to a main course. So, when dining at home, preparing a meal for friends, or simply eating alone, I want lots of small plates, or bites of a variety of things.

Oh! That's already a 'thing'?

Yep! It's called Meze, Tapas, Appetizer, Izakaya, Mezethakia, Antipasto, Hors D' Oeuvre, Dim Sum, depending where you are from. It already exists.

Beautifully, thoughtfully planned small plates can be prepared for any occasion, or we can simply rummage around the fridge or pantry for lots of leftovers, odds and ends, pickled things, smoked things, cheesy things, and don't forget the egg! And keep in mind: it is always wise to keep pastry options in the freezer; such as puffed pastry, phyllo dough, wonton wrappers, eggroll shells, tortillas or small tart shells. A simple bread dough on the day of the gathering also makes for a multitude of options.

Yes. This is my favorite way to eat, and so I want to lure you to my table with lots of creative ways to serve absolutely anything on a small plate.

By the way, did you know the translation of the term Chinese "Dim Sum" is 'little hearts'? I just love that. A wise approach to keeping the ole heart in good condition, don't you think!

When my parents had friends over, when I was a young girl, careful consideration was given to the table arrangements, small plates or bowls, tiny forks, spoons, and knives, and hand embroidered cocktail napkins for the display of Meze. It offered such a variety of options to eat, while sipping on a drink throughout the evening, that nothing else was served other than coffee and dessert.

Sticks. Oh, how I love to put anything on a small stick! Can you believe I even created a Pizza on a Stick? Wooden or metal skewers make it so easy to arrange a platter, and serve straight from the fridge, pop into the oven to warm, or place it on a hot grill just before serving.

I have created many small plate recipes over the years, and now I am excited to share some of them with you!

THE BIRD

··

When you think of Chicken, Hen, or Turkey, what recipe first comes to mind? A big ole plate of meat served solo with after-thought sides? Not me! I envision a multitude of small plates that simply incorporate the delicious and succulent meat from the birds. A vast collection of wraps, sticks, bundles, cups of broth with hidden culinary treasures submerged into a three-bite delight.

Nearly every country in the world incorporates these birds into dishes that show-cases regional ingredients. Two interesting facts that made me laugh, "The only country without live chickens is Vatican City, and the only continent without them is Antarctica". So, that means recipes are endless.

While living in Brazil, I found nearly all meat or fish dishes were best prepared pierced with a sword, heavily salted, and ignited into near flames as it roasted on fire made from strips of dried wood, and bundles of dried aromatic herbs that looked much like stalks of weeds from my back yard, until the aromas rose up, and nearly reached the nostrils of the statue on Corcovado! As for the rest of us, we first have to cook the bird, and infuse it with lots of flavors, and that is where every international cuisine flaunts its unique approach to the plain ole bird.

THE MENU

BASTILLA – CHICKEN ROLLS
FESENJAN – POMEGRANATE CHICKEN
GREEK CHICKEN WRAPS
ITALIAN CHICKEN SOUP CUPS
MAC & CHEESE TURKEY ROLLS
CHICKEN & WAFFLES

NOW that we have a flavor packed heap of carefully cooked and picked bundles of poultry, the recipes that I love most are about to find their place on your plate. Whenever possible, simmer a pot of whole chicken or two, along with fresh herbs, garlic, lemon, and a healthy heaping of salt. The chicken will take on much more flavor, and the broth will also have flavor for any recipe you will need, even if it is simply used for cooking rice. The picked chicken and the broth can be frozen, which cuts down on prep time when you are ready for any of these recipes.

ITALIAN SOUP
SCRAPS

GREEK CHICKEN
LETTUCE WRAPS
CUBED

MOROCCAN
CHICKEN ROLL
SHREDDED

11

CHICKEN ROLLS - BASTILLA

Morocco

My twist on a traditional Moroccan chicken dish. Sometimes, chicken just needs to get all dressed up and look fancy! This Moroccan Chicken Roll recipe takes the underrated chicken and elevates it to a whole new level.

Using the breast meat of a cooked whole chicken, or simply purchase breast of chicken, bake it, or boil it, shred it, and half the work is done.

Once the ingredients are mixed, place the filling in phyllo dough, roll it, bake it, and it will surely wow any guest, or simply feel as though you have treated yourself to a very sophisticated dinner. Don't be intimidated by phyllo dough, it is easy to work and quite forgiving.

Makes 2 logs - 16 slices

- Chicken breast – 1 ½ breast shredded
- Eggs – 3
- Lemon juice – ½ cup
- Almond meal – 1 cup
- Olive oil – 2 tablespoons
- Cinnamon – 1 tablespoon
- Salt – 2 teaspoons
- Garlic – 2 cloves, crushed
- Cayenne pepper – a pinch or to taste
- Powdered sugar and cinnamon mix to dust on top of baked rolls, 1 teaspoon of each
- Slivered almonds – 2 tablespoons sprinkled on top of finished rolls
- Phyllo sheets – 6
- Butter – 3 tablespoons, melted to brush onto phyllo dough

Instruction

In a bowl mix eggs, lemon juice, olive oil, and garlic. Add chicken, spices, and almond meal. Blend until all ingredients are moist. Brush melted butter onto phyllo dough, one sheet at a time until you have stacked 3 layers.

Place half of the filling at one end (long end) of the phyllo sheets, gently roll and brush a little butter as you roll. Place sealed closing down onto parchment paper lined cookie sheet. Do the same with the second roll.

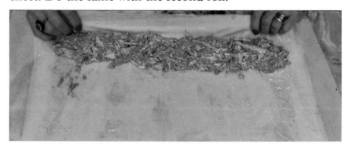

At a diagonal, cut 1/3 way through the roll before baking. Brush any remaining butter across the top. (cutting before baking makes it easier to cut through the crunchy pastry after it is cooked)

Bake 350 for about 35-40 minutes, or until the pastry is golden.

While rolls are still hot, dust the cinnamon/sugar mixture across the tops, sprinkle the slivered almonds, and cut all the way through the rolls.

Moroccan Chicken Roll

Pomegranate Chicken

....

ran

One of my children's favorite fruits, while growing up, was the pomegranate. Growing up in the city of Annapolis, exposure to ethnicity was far more limited than I would have preferred, and the pomegranate was not a fruit eaten by many of their friends. But when autumn arrived, and play time outside was brisk and refreshing, I would often send each of them outside with half of a pomegranate so that they could enjoy the novelty of sucking all the tart juice from each seed, and then spitting the seeds somewhere outside! Fesenjan, this delicious Iranian dish, incorporates many ingredients I would never have thought to put together in a chicken dish: pomegranate molasses, walnuts, and pumpkin.

Serves 8 small cups

- Walnuts – 1 cup, lightly toasted and ground
- Broth – 1 cup for walnut base, 1 cup for chicken base
- Chicken thighs – about 8 (2 cups chopped)
- Oil – 2 tablespoons, walnut oil, or olive oil
- Onions – 2 cups, chopped
- Pumpkin Puree – 2 cups
- Spices – 1 tablespoon of each – salt, pepper, allspice, garlic, turmeric powder, Red pepper flakes – ¼ teaspoon (optional)
- Pomegranate molasses – ¼ cup
- Tri-colored carrots – 3, cut into quarter inch cubes, confetti cut
- Brown Rice – 2 cups of cooked rice

Instruction

Simmer the ground walnuts and ½ cup of water in a small pan until it begins to bubble. Add broth and continue to simmer on low while preparing the chicken.

Saute onions in the oil until they begin to caramelize. Add chicken and brown slightly. Add the pumpkin, spices, broth, and pomegranate molasses. Cover and simmer on low for about 15 minutes. Add walnut sauce, cover and continue simmering for another 40 minutes, adding the carrots the last 5 minutes.

Delicious served over rice and garnished with pomegranate seeds or fresh herbs.

GREEK LETTUCE WRAPS

Greece

While Greece is often thought of as the land of lamb and sea-food, there are actually more chicken dishes than lamb. Lamb Souvlaki and Lamb Gyros used to be a favorite of mine until I had them made with chicken. A delicious alternative to its dominant flavored lamb competition.

Greek salads. Who doesn't love a Greek salad with its lemony fresh flavors of crispy lettuce, cucumbers, olives, and feta cheese! But on this day, I was looking to create a 'mezethakia' (small-plate appetizer) that would showcase a roasted chicken I had on hand, and a Greek salad. The catch? I wanted guests to be able to pick it up by hand! Thus, my Greek Lettuce Wraps were created, and a huge hit!

Makes 4

- Chicken – 2 cups, cooked and cubed
- Bib lettuce – 4 large leaves
- Cucumber – 1 cup, cut into ½ inch cubes
- Plain Greek yogurt – 3 tablespoons
- Black olives – ¼ cup, quartered
- Olive oil – 1 tablespoon
- Lemon juice – 1 tablespoon
- Salt/Pepper to taste
- Oregano – 1 teaspoon chopped plus sprigs for garnish
- Feta – 2 tablespoons, crumbled to place on top of the wrap

Instruction

In a bowl, mix the yogurt, lemon juice, and olive oil. Add chicken, cucumber, olives and spices. Mix well so that all ingredients are moist. Place filling in the lettuce leaf, taco style. Place feta across the top, and you are ready to serve.

Greek Chicken Wraps

Italian Chicken Soup

ITALIAN CHICKEN SOUP CUPS

Italy

Did you know that just about any Italian dish you can think of, can be turned into toppings on a pizza, or made into a soup? Imagine that!

While I am pretty sure my next cookbook will be totally dedicated to pizzas and pastas, and all the unimaginable ways to serve each, today I am in want of something tiny and warm to serve to guests on a small-plate spread. The easy approach to this, is simply make a favorite soup, and serve it in tiny cups, and this is my favorite Italian Chicken Soup.

Makes 6 four-ounce cups
- Chicken pieces – 1 ½ cups, cooked and chopped
- Pasta – 1 cup, small cooked for 8 minutes, finish cooking in soup
- Green beans – 1 cup, chopped into ½ inch pieces
- Mini tomatoes – 1 cup, chopped into ½ inch pieces
- Garlic – 1 clove, crushed
- Basil – 2 tablespoons, freshly chopped
- Salt/Pepper to taste
- Grated cheese – enough to sprinkle when served
- Olive oil – 1 tablespoon to saute vegetables
- Lemon juice – ½ lemon, squeezed
- Chicken broth – 2 cups

Instruction

In a saucepan, add olive oil, lemon juice, green beans, and tomatoes. Saute high and fast. As soon as the green beans begin to take on a brighter green, take it off the heat, and toss. Warm the broth when ready to serve. Add chicken and pasta. Let it get hot but don't boil, remember that everything is cooked. Add the remaining ingredients, stir, and cover until ready to serve. Sprinkle cheese and uncooked chopped basil on top. Delicious with Olive Bread!

MAC & CHEESE TURKEY ROLLS

America

Thanksgiving-In-A-Bite. Imagine that! All the flavors of sage and onions, celery and roasted turkey are encased in a buttery crunchy phyllo dough. Toss together an apple salad, with a few nuts and raisins, serve it in a cabbage leaf, and I would say you have just created a small plate meal that will inspire the craving for that iconic dish we all look forward to every November.

Serves 6

- Gruyere cheese - 1 cup, diced
- Butter - 2 tablespoon, for sauce
- Butter - 3 tablespoons, to baste phyllo dough
- Flour - 2 tablespoons
- Sage - 1 teaspoon, dried
- Turkey broth - 1 cup turkey
- Celery - 1 cup, chopped confetti chop
- Scallions - ½ cup, chopped
- Salt/Pepper - to taste
- Cooked turkey - 2 cups, cut into small pieces
- Macaroni - 2 cups, cooked
- Phyllo dough - 6 sheets

Instruction

On a medium heat, place 2 tablespoon of butter in a pan, add scallions and celery. Toss for a minute then sprinkle flour on the bottom of the pan and stir everything together. Pour broth and continue stirring. Add turkey, seasonings, cheese, and pasta and quickly stir it all together so everything is incorporated and the cheese melts and holds it all together. Turn pan off. This part can be done in advance. Or move on to filling the dough.

Preheat oven to 350. Brush melted butter across phyllo dough, one layer at a time until you have 3 layers stacked and lightly buttered. Lay half the filling mixture at one end and roll it into a log. Place on a baking sheet, preferable parchment paper lined. Repeat the steps to prepare a second log. At a diagonal, cut 1/3 the way into the log, making several slices about 2 inches apart. This makes it easier to slice after it has baked. Bake 25 to 30 minutes until top is golden. Cut the remainder of the way through while warm and serve.

Mac & Cheese Turkey Roll

CHICKEN & WAFFLES

America – Down South

You have not experienced America until you have had Chicke[n] and Waffles! Had it not been for my West Virginia, foodie gir[l] friend, who has collaborated with me on a filmmaking adven[n]ture to showcase our feisty approach to the theme, "60 is the ne[w] 40," I would never have indulged myself in such southern treat[s]. To make these fast, I suggest purchasing ready-made waffles, an[d] pressing them into small-plate size sandwiches, but if you fin[d] yourself with extra time on your hands, you can make a batch o[f] homemade waffles and freeze them to have on hand, those wi[ll] be best. The rest goes fast and delicious!

FRIED CHICKEN – for 6 waffle sandwiches

- Chicken – 2 breasts or 4 thighs, deboned and cut the thickness of ¼ inch
- Flour – 1 cup
- Baking soda – 1 teaspoon
- Salt/Pepper or Chipotle chili powder to taste
- Butter – 3 tablespoons
- Mini tomatoes – 12 (optional)
- Grated cheese – ¼ cup (optional)
- Cucumbers or pickles – ¼ cup, thinly sliced (optional)
- Arugula, Pea shoots, or Shredded cabbage – ½ cup (optional)
- Ghost Chili Maple Syrup – ¼ cup (optional), buy already made or mix your own

Instruction

Once the chicken is cut thin, and then cut again to fit the size of your waffles, toss the flour, baking soda, and seasoning into a bag/baggie, add the chicken and give it a good shake. Place half the butter in a hot skillet and brown the chicken on both sides, in batches, adding more butter as needed. Pop them in a 325 degrees oven for about 15 minutes.

WAFFLES – makes 12 for 6 waffle sandwiches

- Yeast – 1 package
- Water – 1 ½ cups water, tepid but not warmer that 115 degrees
- Sugar – 1 teaspoon
- Flour – 3 cups
- Salt – ½ teaspoon
- Eggs – 3, separated, whip the whites and set aside
- Milk – 1 ½ cups
- Cooked carrots or beets – 2 tablespoons, pureed (optional)
- Butter – 1 stick (8 tablespoons), melted and cooled

Instruction

In a large bowl, stir the yeast and sugar into water, and let sit for 10 minutes. Stir in flour. Mix egg yolks to milk. Add to flour. Stir in the melted butter, salt, and cooked beets/carrots if using. Now fold in the egg whites. Let the mixture stand for 1 hour.

Heat the waffle griddle and make the waffles in batches. The waffles and chicken are ready to assemble. Serve with your favorite sandwich extras!

DINING
AT HOME

Having a little get together, or simply want to enjoy a different dining experience for two? Migrate away from the dining room or kitchen table, dress up an over-looked nook in your home and create a unique dining experience right there in your own home!

It's amazing how many items we collect in our home, forget about, and never use. Low tables, currently being used as end tables, entryway tables or consoles gathering dust and chachka make for the perfect tabletops to gather a few chairs around and create small-plate dining for the evening. Be creative, display interesting conversation pieces, candles, great food, and enjoy your new dining ambiance!

LET'S BREAK
BREAD TOGETHER

Often, when I plan to have a gathering of friends and family, the food that ranks top of the list of dishes I will serve, is bread. Breads are among the most ancient of recipes. It doesn't matter if it is leavened with yeast, unleavened, or in the form of a cracker. There is something therapeutic about working the hands in dough, smelling it bake, and watching it come alive.

Growing up in my home, bread was most often made with wheat, but having visited bakeries in other parts of the world, I have embraced other grains and flour made from things I would never have thought to use: yucca, nuts, rice and on and on.

My favorite bread has always been Olive Rosemary Bread; salty, briny from the olives, and aromatic from the rosemary. It is simply scrumptious! Is it Italian? French? Syrian? Since I created it, I would best say that it was influenced by the flavors of all three cuisines. It comes together by hand quite fast, and it rises within one hour. When I am preparing a table of small plates, this is the bread I will usually make. It can be made into large loaves and served as the base for a bruschetta or made into long thin loaves and sliced thin to serve as a base for savory canapes. The possibilities are endless with homemade bread.

In truth, at the end of a gathering, once everyone has gone, the dishes are done, I am barefoot and sipping a quiet glass of wine before turning in for the night; it is one last slice of Olive Rosemary Bread that I nibble to celebrate the memories of the evening.

THE MENU

OLIVE ROSEMARY BREAD

CAPRESE BITES

CUCUMBER DIP - TZATZIKI

CRAB CAKES

ROSEMARY ROASTED POTATO FRIES

SMALL PLATES:
a medley of smoked fish and cheeses

POMEGRANATE MARTINI

feast

Olive Bread

OLIVE ROSEMARY BREAD

Mediterranean

Makes 1 Large Loaf

- Yeast – 2 teaspoons
- Water – 1 ½ cup
- Salt – 1 teaspoon
- Rosemary – 1 tablespoon freshly chopped
- Grated cheese – ½ cup pecorino (optional)
- Olives – ½ cup, chopped
- Olive oil – ¼ cup
- Flour – 4 to 5 cups
- Egg wash – 1 egg mixed with 1 tablespoon water
- Coarse salt – sprinkled on top

Instruction

Place the yeast, sugar, and water in a bowl and let sit for 10 minutes. Add salt, pepper, rosemary, cheese, olives and olive oil. Mix. Slowly blend in flour.

Oil a clean bowl, and place the dough in the bowl, cover, and let rise till double in size. About one hour.

Punch down, and shape into a bread log, place on a parchment paper lined baking sheet, and brush with egg wash. Sprinkle course sea salt.

Place in a preheated 400 degrees oven. Bake 18 – 20 minutes until top is golden.

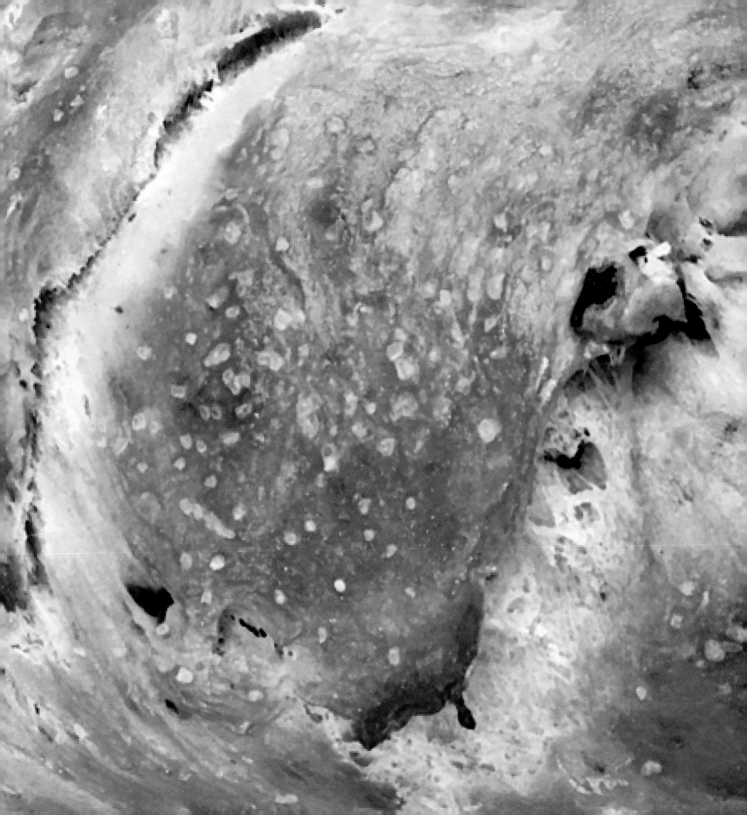

Caprese Bites

CAPRESE BITES – INSALATA CAPRESE

....

Italy

Salad on a stick. Sometimes a little salad on a stick is all we are looking for, says my whimsical imagination! Easy to pack in lunches. Perfect for a Tapas spread, picnic food, or an appetizer for game day when you want your loved-ones, or guests to have a little something healthy. Caprese Bites are a take on the traditional Italian Caprese Salad, which is usually mozzarella, basil, and tomatoes. These are made with spinach and drunken goat cheese and are the perfect solution for a salad without all the mess, not to mention the salad dressing swimming at the bottom of a bowl!

Serves 2

- Cherry tomatoes – 4 to 6, cut in half
- Spinach leaves – 8 to 12
- Drunken Goat Cheese - ¼ pound, cut into half-inch cubes
- Fresh Oregano leaves – 8 to 12
- Toothpicks – 8 to 12
- Olive oil – 1 teaspoon
- Salt to taste

Instruction

Place a toothpick through the cheese cubes first. (I chose this cheese because it's semi-soft and will not crumble when inserting a tooth-pick, but mozzarella is good too). Next slide the halved tomato, then the spinach leaf, and place the tiny oregano leaf on top of the cheese. Place these lovelies on a plate, drizzle a little olive oil, and sprinkle a little salt and they are ready. An easy do-ahead.

Tzatziki

CUCUMBER DIP – TZATZIKI

Greece

Cucumbers. The often-forgotten vegetable. Or is it a fruit? None the less, I love its fresh versatile flavor. The cool refreshing flavor of Tzatziki comes to the aid of spicy food, calms the tummy after a heavy meal, and makes for a perfect tapas dish for any cuisine you are serving.

This Greek salad, or side dish, is a staple in my home all summer. I grew up eating it with meats the way many Americans put ketchup on theirs. Make up a batch and keep it in the fridge for a few days. Have it on your kabobs, grilled chicken, roasted eggplant, lamb, veggie kabobs, or use it as a salad dressing. Fast, easy, and oh so yummy!

Makes 2 cups

- Cucumber – 2 cups, skin on, thinly sliced, and quartered
- Lemon juice and zest – from 1 lemon
- Thick Greek Yogurt – 2 cups
- Fresh Mint – 2 tablespoons, finely chopped
- Olive oil – 2 teaspoons
- Kosher or Smoked Salt – to taste

Instruction

Mix all ingredients together and serve. Can be made in advance but, wait to add the mint just before serving. Garlic or raw onions can also be added as an option.

CRAB CAKES

Maryland

No one visits the east coast, particularly Maryland, without retaining the memories of the best Crab Cakes they've ever had! What I am about to share with you, comes from a long line of Marylander's rarely straying from this ingredient combination.

Makes 12 small crab cakes

- Lump Crab Meat – 1 pound
- Mayonnaise – 1 tablespoon
- Egg – 1
- Old Bay Seasoning – 1 tablespoon
- Lemon juice – ½ tablespoon
- Salt – to taste
- Butter – 2-3 tablespoons, as needed to saute

Instruction

Gently mix all the ingredients, except the butter. Form small balls. In a medium hot pan, so as not to burn the butter, saute until golden in color, both sides of the crab cakes, adding butter after each batch as needed. Flatten just a little if you are serving these on a cracker or leave them in a ball shape to serves as crab balls. No sauce is needed. These are divine as they are!

Crab Cakes
Photo by Jackie Matera

Rosemary Roasted Potato Frie.

ROSEMARY ROASTED POTATO FRIES

Have you ever been served one baked potato and wondered if you could really eat the whole thing? Yet, two whole Rosemary Roasted Potato Fries set before you, and you will be in want of more! Potatoes are funny like that.

The recipe for these wicked good potatoes couldn't be easier. Russet potatoes, with their thicker skin, make for the crunchiest potato fries, but honestly, if you have a hankering for fries, any potatoes already in your fridge will be delicious.

Serves 4

- Potatoes – 2 per person, cut into long wedges about ½ inch thick
- Olive Oil – 1-2 tablespoons, enough to lightly coat
- Rosemary – freshly chopped, the more the better
- Salt – 1 or more tablespoons of coarse salt (the crunch is best with coarse salt)
- Non-Stick cooking spray (optional) or rub a little olive oil on the pan

Instruction

Preheat oven to 425

Lightly oil a baking sheet.

Toss potato wedges in a bowl with oil, rosemary, and salt.

Arrange on the pan so that they are not piled on top of each other. Roast for about 20 minutes. Turn oven to Broil, and broil for 3-5 minutes, but watch closely so they don't burn.

POMEGRANATE MARTINI

Who needs a holiday to enjoy a great martini! While I am most proficient popping the cork on a bottle of wine or champagne, I really know very little about mixing cocktails, and so I invited my niece, a very talented mixologist who also happens to be a wedding planner, to show me how this drink comes together.

Makes 2

- Pomegranate Vodka – 4 shots
- Cranberry juice – 3 shots
- Pomegranate juice – 1 shot
- Lime juice – from 1 lime
- Rosemary sprigs with 2 whole cranberries on the sprig, for garnish.
- Ice & Shaker

Instruction

Fill the shaker half full, with ice. Add vodka, and both juices. Place the lid on and give a good shake. Pour into the martini glasses and squeeze half a lime in each glass. Garnish.

Pomegranate Martini

ANNIVERSARY 911

Whether you're into numbers or not, you might be intrigued to know that the numbers 911 are iconic. In numerology, it is said that 911 represents the Angel Number: A real friend is one who walks in when the rest of the world walks out.

For those of you who know me, you know I raised my four beautiful children from a collision of life experiences, as a single mom. For those of you who do not know me, I will tell you now, being a single mom is one of life's most difficult jobs, and one that requires selflessness and a whole lotta love!

Once my children were finally old enough to go out into the world on their own and begin to make their mark in life, I decided it was ok, and certainly time, for mama to carve out a life of her own.

Marriage presented itself for me, to one of life's last chivalrous men, and so I took the plunge. Different as night and day in absolutely every way, we had a few rather unique common threads that inspired me enough to take the plunge; we were both well-traveled, bilingual, appreciative of ethnicity, and old enough to just be friends if that was as good as it got.

I jumped in, and it has been a breath of fresh air. An angel visitation, as it were. And the date we eloped to Bermuda, was 911!

Our six-year mark has just passed and if you know anything about Maryland, where we live, you know September is a fickle month when it comes to the weather. And so, for our anniversary celebration I decided to enjoy dining outside, before the chill set in, have a back-up firepit, and a variety of our favorite tapas!

What might we each like, in the way of food you might ask, since we are both lovers of ethnic cuisines? That is a walloping good question! My travels have exposed me primarily to Italy, Greece, Portugal, many Caribbean islands, and a three-year residency in Brazil. Hubby, on the other hand, has been just about everywhere, except South America and the Caribbean, and he lived and worked for thirty years in Hong Kong, where he dined on the culinary treasures of numerous Asian countries. So, what am I going to cook? That is the beauty of small plate dining, we can have everything!

THE MENU

CAVIAR BLINIS

BRUSSELS SPROUT SLIDERS

GHOST CHILI ONION JAM

LAMB TENDERLOINS

SMALL PLATES:

a medley of fruit and spiced yams

SPELT BREAD

Caviar Blinis

BEET ROOT BLINIS

Russia

When I was a little girl, my first girlfriend's mother was from Russia. Being Russian Orthodox, her mama shared many traditions with my Syrian Orthodox mother. Food, of course, was one of them.

Later in life, during my teen-age, child-rearing years, my girlfriend was Ukrainian. We too shared so many traditions together, my favorite being the food! She and her daughter would spend days in the kitchen preparing Borscht, Perogies, and Stuffed Cabbage, have my kids and I over for a special occasion dinner, and share many stories about her heritage.

These Beet Root Blinis I created, are a concoction made to capture the beautiful color of borscht into a mini pancake and indulge my hubby with some caviar. Hope you love them!

BLINIS - Makes 24

- Dry Yeast – 2 teaspoons
- Sugar – 1 teaspoon
- Flour – 1 cup
- Kefir – 1 cup (yogurt can substitute)
- Eggs – 2, separated
- Cooked Beet – 1 golf ball size, pureed
- Prepared Horseradish – 1 tablespoon
- Salt – to taste, about ½ teaspoon
- Butter – to cook blinis, about 1 tablespoon

CAVIAR BLINIS & MASCARPONE

Instruction

Mix yeast, sugar, and flour in a bowl. Warm the kefir, only to tepid temperature, (not warmer than 112 degrees). Stir egg yolks into the tepid kefir and stir into the flour mixture. Let this batter rest for one hour.

Whip the egg whites, mix in horseradish, and pureed beets. Fold this mixture into the flour mixture and let rest one hour.

Place small amounts of butter at a time into a non-stick frying pan. Spoon in 1 tablespoon of batter at a time until you can fit several into the pan. As soon as bubbles begin to form on the top, flip them over for another minute, and remove from the pan. Place on a cooling rack and continue to make the blinis.

The blini can be made several days ahead of time and kept in an airtight container in the fridge. As an extra added measure of protection for keeping the blinis, I like to cut small squares of parchment paper to place between each blini.

Makes 12

- Mascarpone – 3/4 cup
- Caviar – 1 ounce
- Chives – 1 bundle, freshly chopped
- Blini – 12, small

Instruction

Place a small dollop, (heaping teaspoon size) of mascarpone in the center of each blini. Place an even smaller dollop of caviar, (using a wooden spoon, or chop stick, never metal) in the center of the mascarpone. Place a sprinkle of chives across the blinis and serve soon after preparing.

Caviar Blinis & Mascarpone

BRUSSELS SPROUTS SLIDERS

America

I was never a fan of cabbage or brussels sprouts growing up. It wasn't until my granddaughter was visiting and helping me sort through some giant brussels sprouts I found in the market, did I decide to make something memorable out of them. Now, when I prepare my Brussels Sprout Sliders, I will always remember that day in my kitchen in which her little hands were smaller that the brussels sprouts!

The preparation for this dish can be easily done in advance and assembled quickly when ready to serve. The Ghost Chili Onion Jam gives this dish the kick they need to elevate layers of flavor, and once I have made up a batch of this jam, I will admit, I begin to put it on everything. It's so darn good!

Makes 2 dozen
- Ghost Chili Onion Jam – ¼ cup, (recipe follows)
- Brussels sprouts – 24, cut in half on a horizontal cut
- Olive oil – 2 tablespoons
- Salt and Pepper – to taste
- Smoked chili flakes – 1 teaspoon
- Bacon - 10 slices
- Brie – 4 oz.
- Toothpicks – 24

Instruction

Preheat oven to 350

In a bowl, toss cut Brussels sprouts, olive oil, salt and pepper. Roast on a baking sheet about 25 minutes, until softened but still maintaining their bright color.

Cook bacon until brown but still soft enough to pierce with a toothpick. Cool, and cut into squares.

Cut brie into ¼ inch thick slices, and then into squares. The idea is to cut the bacon and cheese into sizes that fit between 2 ends of Brussels sprouts, leaving a little showing.

Place one end of the Brussels sprout on the toothpick, a piece of bacon, then cheese, a quarter teaspoon of onion jam, and finish with the bottom Brussels sprout end. Place on a platter and sprinkle smoked chili flakes across.

Serve room temperature or pop in the oven for just one minute, but do not melt the cheese. These will store a day or two in the fridge.

Brussels Sprout Sliders

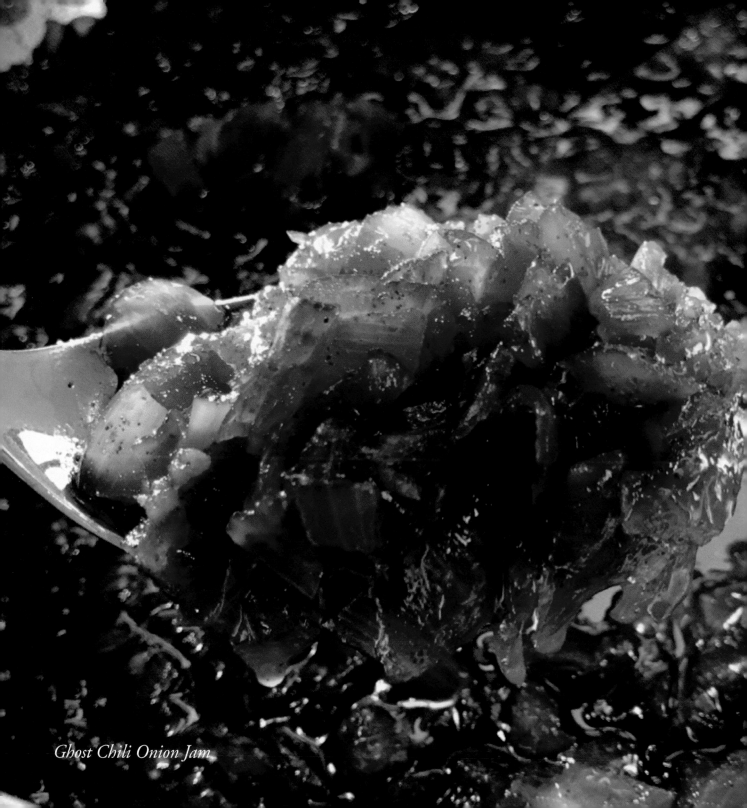

Ghost Chili Onion Jam

GHOST CHILI ONION JAM

America

Makes 12 ounces

- Onions – 4 medium, finely chopped
- Butter – 4 tablespoons
- Brown sugar – 1/3 cup
- Maple syrup – 3 tablespoons
- Garlic cloves – 3, crushed
- Vinegar of your choice – 3 tablespoons
- Smoked chili powder – 2 teaspoons
- Salt – 2 teaspoons
- Ghost Chili – A pinch or two, or at your own risk!

Instruction

Melt butter in a saute pan. Add onions and cook them down until soft. Add remaining ingredients and simmer on medium until the sauce thickens and becomes ooey gooey-like. Cool and store in a glass jar in the fridge.

ROSEMARY LEMON LAMB TENDERS

Syria

The only way I have ever flavored lamb, has been with rosemary and lemon. I thought, growing up, it was the way it was done, until I went out into the world and discovered every cuisine has its own twist on flavoring lamb. But for me, it is rosemary and lemon, because that's the way my Syrian mama did it!

Lamb tenderloins are something you might have to ask your local butcher to cut for you on the day lamb is brought into their market. Just like beef tenderloin, this strip of meat is most desirable, simply because it's pure meat; no bones, very little fat, and no marbling inside the strip. This makes it tender, but also means it needs a little extra help with flavors.

This Lamb Bruschetta style plate is a beautiful way to showcase such a delicate piece of meat. I marinate them in rosemary, salt, lemon, and olive oil, and then sear them on all sides in a hot cast iron pan. Let is rest, slice it thin, and serve on top of a thin slice of bread, and a drizzle of the pan juices.

Serves 4

- Rosemary – 3 sprigs, freshly chopped and lay covering both sides of the lamb
- Lemon juice and zest – 1 tablespoon
- Olive oil – 1 tablespoon, drizzled on both sides which will also act as the fat when you pop the meat onto a searing hot pan
- Salt – to taste
- Lamb tenderloins – about 1 pound

Instruction

Sear on all sides. Cook only until rare. Remove the lamb from the heat and let it rest for a good 10 minutes before slicing very thin. Serve on my Spelt Bread or thinly sliced baguette.

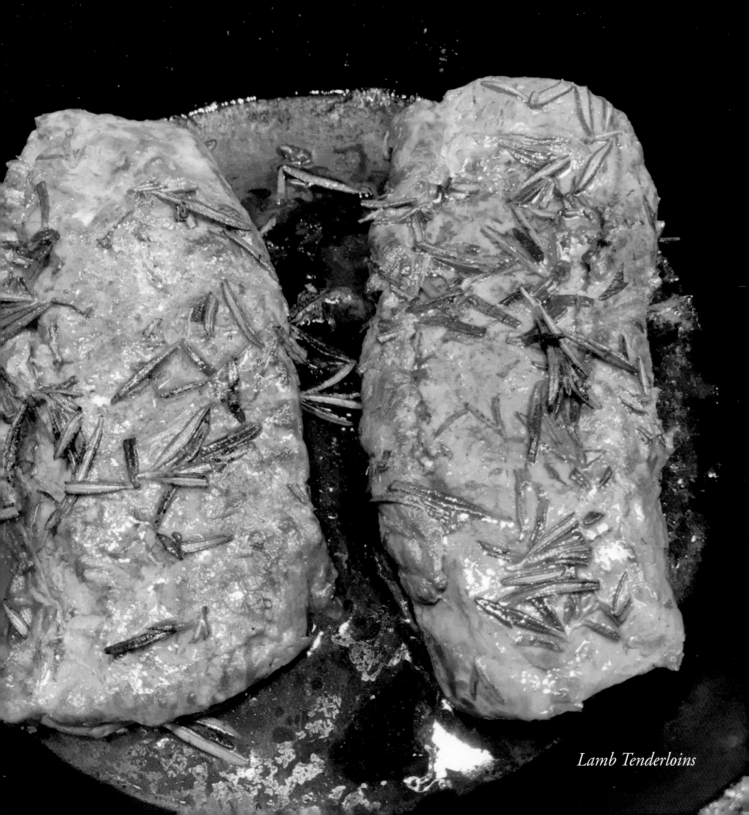

Lamb Tenderloins

Spelt Bread
Photo by Ana Fallon Photography

SPELT BREAD

Makes 1 loaf

- Yeast – 2 teaspoons
- Sugar – 1 tablespoon
- Water – ½ cup
- Kefir – 1 ½ cups
- Spelt flour - 4 to 5 cups, as needed to bring dough to a firm ball
- Olive oil – 1 tablespoon
- Salt – 1 tablespoon

Instruction

Preheat oven to 400.

Mix yeast, sugar, and water together and let sit five minutes to dissolve yeast.

Add kefir, oil, and a little flour and stir to make a batter.

Add salt, and slowly fold in flour, stirring until it becomes too stiff to stir, of which you begin to work it with your hands, adding flour and kneading until dough is no longer sticky.

Cover in an oiled bowl and let sit in a warm (not hot) place until it rises. Usually about 1 hour.

Shape the bread or place in a loaf pan. Brush a little oil or egg-wash on top and bake about 20 minutes.

Izakaya

JAPAN • IZAKAYA

It was 1980 when the film Shogun, was released. I was captivated. I got this feeling that a minimalist philosophy didn't translate as less, in the lives of the Japanese, but rather more. Few words, said more. Fewer things, felt rich. Less on a plate was actually, magically infused with more. I immediately immersed myself in Japanese culture, for a side trip in life!

I began language classes at The Japan America Society in DC. Went to Samurai foreign films. Frequented Japanese restaurants and enjoyed experimenting with Japanese food in my own kitchen.

Izakaya intrigued me. I grew up on Meze; the Middle Eastern style of multiple small plate dining. I was enthusiastic to embrace Izakaya; the Japanese style of small plate dining.

By 1981, I was with child, and yes, I gave my firstborn a Japanese name. But that story is 'film-material' for another time.

Before we get started, I want to be certain we are all on the same well-informed page about Japanese food. The word Sushi simply means 'vinegar rice' and Sashimi is the word for raw fish. There is so much more to Japanese cuisine than this! There are a vast variety of dishes with noodles. Lots of marinated items on a stick and roasted over fire, even if the fire is just a small tabletop hibachi. Oh, and speaking of fire roasting foods, I discovered, while living in Brazil, that the largest number of Japanese living outside Japan, are in Brazil! Must be that fire-roasting on a large open fire, or the sometimes, primitive looking indoor cooking arrangements, where-by a wood fire could be built in what appears to be an oven with open burners on top. While it may look primitive, it was a fabulous way to cook food!

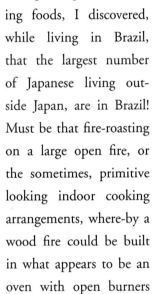

THE MENU

SQUID WITH SQUID INK NOODLES
TOFU AND BEAN SPROUT SALAD
CHILI CHICKEN YAKITORI
ANCHOVY SALAD & SHICHIMI TOGARASHI
STEAK YAKITORI
BLUE MOON

SQUID WITH SQUID INK NOODLES

This is an easy and favored dressing for squid served as a cold dish.

Serves 4 to 6
- Squid – 1 pound
- Squid Ink Pasta or Buckwheat Pasta – ½ pound cooked and cooled

Instruction

Simply sear the squid pieces in a tablespoon of oil, toss, and as soon as they become firm and a bit pink, take them off the heat, cool, and slice into bite size pieces and toss in this dressing.

Dressing

- Coconut milk – ¼ cup
- Lime juice – 2 tablespoons
- Coconut oil – 1 tablespoon
- Garlic – 2 cloves, crushed
- Chili peppers – a pinch
- Fish sauce – 1 teaspoon

Instruction

In a separate bowl, make this same dressing and toss the noodles in it. Serve the pasta along-side of the squid, with a shaved pickled ginger.

Double the recipe, mix in advance and have ready to toss with squid and noodles.

Squid With Squid Ink Noodles

Tofu & Bean Sprout Salad

TOFU & BEAN SPROUT SALAD

Serves 4 to 6

- Firm Tofu – 12 oz block, cut into ½ inch squares
- Bean Sprout Salad – Recipe here
- Sesame oil – 2 tablespoons
- Soy sauce – 1 ½ teaspoons
- 7 Spice Powder – 1 ½ teaspoons, buy or make your own: 1 teaspoon each of dried chili powder, sesame seeds, dried orange peel, salt, and kelp granules
- Black sesame seeds – 1 teaspoon
- Fresh bean sprouts – 1 pound

Instruction

Bring a pot of water to a boil. Drop in Bean Sprouts, toss, remove quickly, run under cold water and drain. In a bowl mix sesame oil, soy sauce, and 7 spice powder. Add sprouts and toss until they are fully coated.

Arrange tofu squares on a plate. Place a tiny mound of sprout salad on top of each square. Sprinkle with black sesame seeds. Serve.

CHILI CHICKEN YAKITORI

Serves 6

- Chicken breast – 1 pound, cut into very thin strips (bacon looking size)
- Soy sauce – ¼ cup
- Mirin (rice vinegar) – ¼ cup
- Sake (or dry white wine) – ¼ cup
- Sugar – 2 tablespoons
- Sesame oil – 1 tablespoon, preferably light sesame oil and not toasted
- Garlic cloves – 2, crushed
- Fresh ginger – 1 tablespoon, minced
- Chili pepper flakes – ¼ teaspoon (or more if you like the heat)
- Scallions – 2 finely chopped for garnish

Instruction

With short bamboo skewer sticks, weave the strips of meat in and out of the stick so they are securely positioned on the sticks.

In a small saucepan bring the sauce ingredients to a simmer and cook low for about 5 minutes, and cool. Reserve ¼ cup of the sauce for serving. Pour the remainder over the chicken in a shallow pan, cover and allow to marinate until ready to cook.

Place on a hot iron pan, grill, or griddle, for about 8 minutes on each side until done. Serve drizzled with reserved sauce and sprinkle with scallions.

Chili Chicken Yakitori

Anchovy Salad & Shichimi Togarashi

ANCHOVY SALAD & SHICHIMI TOGARASHI

Serves 4 to 6

- Anchovies - about one pound, packaged in vinegar, and drained
- Schichimi Togarashi (7 spice powder) - 2 teaspoons, easily made at home: a quick method to make is simply mix 1 teaspoon each of dried chili powder, sesame seeds, dried orange peel, salt, and kelp granules.
- Sesame oil - 1 tablespoon
- Sake or dry white wine - 1 tablespoon
- Daikon - 2 cups, shredded
- Peas shoots or micro greens - ½ cup

Instruction

In a shallow bowl, mix the spice mixture, oil, and sake. Gently toss in anchovies until each is lightly coated. Serve in a small, yet impressive mound, with a bundle of pea shoots and a cluster of daikon. This salad has spicy yet refreshing flavors together!

STEAK YAKITORI

If you are lucky enough to have already made a jar of the Ghost Chili Onion Jam, the rest of this recipe goes fast. If not, take a moment to prepare the jam recipe and let it simmer while you slice the beef and place it on skewers.

Serves 4 to 6
- Skirt Steak – 1 pound, cut into bacon-like strips
- Ghost Chili Onion Jam – ½ cup, Recipe found in Anniversary 911

Instruction

With small bamboo skewers or long appetizer toothpicks that have been soaking in water, so they don't burn, weave the meat strips onto the skewers. Remember these are for small plates, so you will only want a one, to two-bite amount placed on the skewer.

On a hot grill, pan, or griddle, sear the beef quickly on both sides, until cooked but still a little pink. Place the meat sticks on a serving dish and spoon a thin layer of the onion jam on top of the beef. These can be served room temperature but are most delicious hot!

Steak Yakitori

Blue Moon Cocktai

BLUE MOON COCKTAIL

While Japan is thought of as the Land of the Rising Sun, I wanted to create a cocktail for this Japanese dining experience that instead celebrated what appears to be Japan's blood moon on its flag. The Blue Moon, The Blood Moon, The Super Moon. Each are rare and unique, and so this cocktail is my whimsical toast to a country whose culture I hold in high esteem.

Serves 2

- Vodka – 2 shots
- Blue Curacao – 1 shot
- Coconut milk – ½ cup plus 2 tablespoons for the simple syrup
- Sugar – 1 tablespoon
- Cardamom seeds – 3
- Orange rind – for garnish, peeled in a ¼ inch strip and speared with a kabob stick
- Ice – ½ cup
- Shaker
- Small pan

Instruction

In a small hot pan, lightly toast the seeds, crushing them as they warm. Sprinkle sugar across the seeds, stir, and watch closely so as not to burn. Pour 2 tablespoons of coconut milk into the pan and remove quickly from heat. Stir, strain, and set aside fo r cocktail time.

Place ice in a shaker cup. Add vodka, curacao, spicy simple syrup, and coconut milk. Give a good shake, pour, and place orange rind garnish across the top.

WHIMSICAL
THE CALIFORNIA INFLUENCE

Nothing captures my attention faster than the unexpected in art. That goes for food as well. I think it is why I am often awestruck with molecular gastronomy. While I don't know how to do this form of food preparation, my eyes twinkle at the thought of enjoying a cocktail presented to me in the form of cotton candy, or a dessert presented in the form of a balloon, then eaten after it first bursts in my face. Whimsical!

I am primarily an east coast girl, though in recent years my book-end children, (oldest and youngest) have become Cali-Kids, and lovers of weird and whimsical food. My two middle children, in contrast, my feet-on-the-ground sons, and daddies still prefer the homecooked ethnic foods I raised them on. My book-ends have sought to take mama off the deep end, into the world of 'free'. Gluten-free, dairy-free, sugar-free, and sometimes meat-free.

Being the good mama that I am, I wanted dining experiences at home to remain something special for all my children when they are home with me. This challenge became a whimsical enlightenment in my kitchen.

While I have always been a health conscience foodie, dating back to the hippie era, making and growing what I could myself; the Cali influence inspired me to take foods I already knew and loved, and turn them into something of a conversation piece, and still taste amazing.

THE MENU

SPAGHETTI CARBONARA
STEAK & ZUCCHINI ROLL-UPS
CASHEW CHEESE TARTS
BLACK BEAN TORTE
CRAB TOWERS
EGG SALAD BITES

ITALY/NYC

I will never forget that cold December morning in 1997, one week before my birthday, when I woke my four children, (ages 8 to 16 at the time) for school, or so they thought. Little did they know the night before, while they were sleeping, I made arrangements. The kind of arrangements only an adventure seeking mom makes on a typical school day. "Kids," I said, "Mama wants you to go empty out your school backpacks and carefully pack enough cloths for a three-day excursion." You would think they might look at their mother as though she had lost her mind, but they knew better.

I had booked train tickets to New York City, and by 9:00 am we were on it. After all, isn't New York the only place to go, weeks before Christmas? The store windows were dressed as though each one would partake in a Hollywood movie. Some of the buildings had ginormous red bows tied around them. I had arranged a hotel room that would accommodate all five of us in one suite, not far from Central Park. Bought tickets to see Cats on Broadway, knowing my cousin was the pianist for the production, would be able to take us backstage at intermission. A midnight ride on a horse-drawn carriage through Central Park, (my two teen-aged sons were not thrilled about that). A surprise excursion my children would never forget, particularly after having just come through an unfortunate domestic situation. They needed this, we all did!

We arrived at about lunch time. Checked into our hotel and then took a cab to Chinatown. It began to snow. How magical, we all thought! We walked up and down the streets and ally-ways of Chinatown looking for something yummy to eat. There were eels swimming around in water baths along the sidewalk. Whole chickens, (un-plucked) hanging upside down from store awnings. Weird smells coming from basement entry shops, one after another. Nothing looked appetizing, and by then we were famished.

We arrived at the end of the street and low and behold, across the street was Little Italy! No one said a word. Arms locked together, like a barrier no one could pass through, we scurried over to Little Italy, chose the first restaurant with tablecloths, brushed off the snow, went inside and ordered the same, exact thing: Spaghetti Carbonara! In short, bacon and eggs folded sensuously into spaghetti!

My new California state of mind? I wanted to detour from the spaghetti carbonara I knew and loved and went on a Whimsical adventure of a different sort. I created a delicious version of an old-faithful! The saltiness of the bacon is there, only I used anchovies. The dreaminess of eggs, though I went for a barely boiled egg yolk, and of course pasta, I chose to compliment the anchovies with squid ink pasta, black. In search of the perfect one-bite delight, I served this old-faithful in a tiny plate, and it looked like a piece of art. I promise you will love it!

Little Italy in New York City will always hold special memories of Italy for us, even though we too have been to Italy numerous times xo

From this day forth, I vowed to live an exceptional life with my four children... and we have!

SPAGHETTI CARBONARA

Italy Meets California

Serves 6

- Squid ink pasta – ½ pound
- Olive oil – 2 tablespoons
- Garlic – 1 clove, crushed
- Dry white wine – 2 tablespoons
- Soft boiled eggs – 6, (5-minute boil, immerse in cold water, and peel immediately)
- Anchovies – 6, (preferably from Spain, aged, and packed in salt and olive oil)

Instruction

In a pan, (large enough to accommodate the pasta once it is cooked) place the olive oil, garlic, and wine. Turn the pan on low, and bring to a slow simmer, just to warm the liquid. Meanwhile cook pasta to al dente, drain, and place in the warm bath of oil and wine and toss to coat the pasta. (We don't want the pasta swimming in the liquids, just to coat with a hint of their flavor.)

Assemble: Twirl about 3 long noodles tightly on a fork, into a gathered ball of pasta and place in the center of your small dish. Place one anchovy per pasta bundle in the center of the pasta, tail sticking up. Gently remove the yolk from the soft-boiled egg and slice a tiny sliver from the yolk so it will stay put on the plate and not roll around. Brush a little of the liquid from the pasta across the egg and serve.

Spaghetti Carbonara –
Ana Fallon Photography

Steak & Zucchini Roll-Ups -
Photo By Ana Fallon Photography

STEAK & ZUCCHINI ROLL-UPS

I can't think of a better way to lure a man into dining off small plates than to serve him steak! These convenient little bundles of dinner in a bite, can be made specifically for this dish, or can be an after-thought when you have grilled way too much steak poolside. Once these bundles are assembled, they can be placed a second time on the grill to char the zucchini, or simply served room temperature. If you are lucky enough to have leftovers, they are perfect to pop into a loved one's lunchbox!

My poor (hah, lucky) kids were often sent to school with the weirdest lunches of the entire school! Like I said earlier, I love anything on a stick and find it such a tidy, yet whimsical way to serve food to children… or, anyone, for that matter!

Makes a dozen

- Skirt steak - 1 pound, marinated on both sides in salt and a drizzle of olive oil
- Zucchini - 3 medium size, cut lengthwise into 1/8-inch slivers
- Lemon - 1, juice and zest
- Olive oil - 1 tablespoon
- Fresh herb, such as basil or cilantro - 12 sprigs
- Toothpicks - 12

Instruction

In a flat pan, fill half way with water, a pinch of salt, and bring to a boil. Place zucchini strips in, count to 20 and pull them out, and rinse in cold water. Lay them flat on a rack or on parchment paper. Once the zucchini drains, toss them in a bowl with the lemon and oil.

If your steak is not yet cooked, simply heat up a cast iron pan until smoking hot, (or your griddle, or grill) toss the steak on, 5 minutes on one side, 1 minute on the other and pull it off. Let it rest. Then cut it into 3-inch long by 1-inch wide strips.

Assemble

Lay zucchini strip on a plate or parchment paper, place a piece of steak, (sticking out) and one sprig of herb onto one end of zucchini. Roll the zucchini gently up and put a tooth pick through it to hold it into place, as well as give the guest something to pick up their bundle with and take a hearty bite!

LEAH TEACHES MAMA!

Call me kooky, but I made these for a Halloween dinner party, and they were a hit! Inspired by my daughter, who wanted non-dairy cheese, (don't knock it till you try these yummies). And so, I concocted my very first cashew cheese at the instruction of my daughter, which is now a regular in my home for spreads, dips, and lots of other Cali influenced dishes! Thank you, Leah, for teaching mama that healthy, no… really healthy food, can be delicious!

CASHEW CHEESE TARTS

Makes 12
- Mini tart shells – 12, found in the freezer section
- Olive oil – 2 tablespoons, for brushing the tart shells
- Anchovies or Sardines –12, one per tart
- Micro greens for garnish

Ingredients for Cashew Cheese -
Makes 2 cups of cheese paste
- Raw cashews, 2 cups, soaked in water for 1 hour, and drained
- White balsamic vinegar – 1 tablespoon
- White pepper – ¼ teaspoon
- Salt – 1 teaspoon
- Lemon juice – 2 tablespoons
- Garlic – 2 cloves, crushed
- Nutritional yeast – 1 tablespoon
- Fenugreek powder – 1 teaspoon
- Water – ¼ cup

Instruction

Place all the cashew cheese ingredients in a blender and puree into a paste. Chill.

Tart assembly

Place tart shells on a baking sheet (preferably with parchment paper under). Brush a little olive oil on tart shells. Bake in a 350 oven for about 5 minutes, just to turn golden. But watch them because they can go from golden to burnt quickly. Let the tarts shells cool 5 minutes.

Place a dollop of cheese in each tart shell. Stand the anchovy into the cheese, tail up, (trimming some of the head end if necessary, to adjust their height). Garnish with a micro-green leaf.

Cashew Cheese Tarts

BRAZIL

I have so much to say about the three years I lived in Brazil, but suffice it to say now, that I found the influence in food, to be as diverse as here in America, with one exception: African cooking. The Afro-Brazilian community makes up more than 50 percent of the Brazilian population. In fact, the national dish of Brazil, Feijoada (beans), has its origins in the country's history with slavery. This dish was first a concoction of the discarded parts of the pig, simmered low and slow, and made into a stew with black beans, other vegetables, and served with rice and other typical Brazilian ingredients.

My oldest son was the first to move to Brazil. I followed and shared in the Brazilian adventure for a few years with him. His language skills as well as his Brazilian cuisine cooking skills are something he continues to celebrate, as he has become my Cali-kid. I created this whimsical dish for him as a reminder of the rich adventures we shared for a snap-shot moment in our lives, together.

Black Bean Torte

BLACK BEAN TORTE

Black Bean Paste

- Black bean – 2/ 15 oz cans
- Salt – 1 teaspoon
- Olive oil – 1 tablespoon
- Red chili flakes – ¼ teaspoon
- Garlic – 2 cloves, crushed
- Teriyaki sauce – 1 tablespoon

Instruction

Puree all ingredients

Assemble

Spread the Black Bean Paste onto each crepe layer, making sure to go all the way to the edges. Stack five layers of crepes with paste, leaving the top crepe without paste. (This can also be done a few hours before serving.)

Cut the torte into rectangular slices to fit the size small plates you are using, and about ¾ inch wide. When ready to serve, place the slices on a platter, making sure to expose the lovely layers.

CRAB TOWERS

Maryland to California

Whether they are Maryland Blue Crabs, or California Dungeness Crabs, Crabs are enjoyed by every seafood lover.

Whether they are served in a messy heap, piled high on a spread of newspapers with beer, crackers and a mallet, sure to splatter your face with their spicy juice, or carefully picked and made into Maryland's infamous Crab Cakes, accompanied by champagne or a crisp Vino Verde. There is no other seafood quite like crabs.

And so, for a lady's luncheon on a warm summer afternoon, I chose to prepare a crab dish I stole from my Executive Chef son Omar, one of Maryland's most diverse chefs. The dish showcases the flavors one might find in a tequila cocktail, or the jalapeno bite of a mango salsa, but the colors are that of summer, to remind us that these moody creatures hide in the warm mud during winter, only to show their face in the light of summer's sun.

Makes 4 large Towers

Crab Preparation
- Lump Crab Meat – 1 pound
- Mayonnaise – 2 tablespoons
- Capers – ¼ cup
- Lemon juice – 1 tablespoon
- Old Bay Seasoning – 1 tablespoon
- Salt – to taste
- Mix and set aside
- Mango Salsa Preparation
- Mangos – 2 cut into tiny cubes

- Jalapeno – 2 or 3, depending on how hot you would like it
- Lime Juice – 1 fresh lime
- Cilantro – ½ cup finely chopped
- Red onion – ¼ cup finely chopped
- Salt – to taste
- Mix and set aside
- Avocado Preparation
- Ripe Avocado – 2 chopped finely
- Lemon or lime juice – 1 freshly squeezed
- Salt to taste
- Mix and set aside

Tower Preparation

While you can use a biscuit or cookie cutter/press, a Sushi Tower Gadget is the easy way to go and they are very affordable! Simply place the press or tower tool on the plate. Stack the three prepared dishes (crab, mango and avocado) one layer at a time. Press all layers down to pack them together, and gently remove the tower form, and you have a beautiful,

Crab Towers

Egg Salad Bites

EGG SALAD BITES

....

Makes 12
- Eggs – 6, hard boiled, peeled, cut in half
- Beets – 1 cup, cooked
- Mascarpone – 2 tablespoons
- Garlic – 1 clove, crushed
- Olive oil – 1 tablespoon
- Avocado – 1 very soft
- Lemon juice – 1 tablespoon
- Salt – to taste
- Black sesame seeds – 1 teaspoon, (optional)

Instruction

In a food processor or blender puree the beets, mascarpone, garlic, olive oil, 3 egg yolks and salt to taste. Transfer this mixture into a piping bag, or a zip bag with one corner snipped just enough to squeeze beet mixture out.

In a clean food processor or blender puree the avocado, lemon juice, 3 egg yolks and salt to taste. Transfer this mixture into a separate piping bag or zip bag with one corner snipped enough to squeeze avocado mixture out.

Set the 12 egg white halves on a tray. Pipe a little beet mixture in the cavity, then a little avocado mix on top. Repeat with all eggs until each is filled. Sprinkle tops with black sesame seeds. Beautiful and tasty!

SISTERS

My Sisters: The oldest living loves of my life. As different as salt and pepper, peanut butter and jelly. Collectively we leave no stone unturned when it comes to rooting out ideas, answers, and our creative approach to life.

We have gathered our own culinary preferences over the years, formed by extensive travel, and lifestyle influences. Each of us has searched for the elixirs that will keep us forever young. We eat, dine, cook, entertain, and even raised our children and grandchildren on a variety of culinary variations.

But when we get together and want to share a family event, or sister's weekend, the comfort food we all hanker for, is that which our mama cooked. The foods that embrace the rich roots of our heritage.

The foods of Syria and the surrounding Mediterranean were spread across our table, in our humble home, on any given occasion worthy to be called a celebration. A time to ignite a scurry of excitement in our kitchen for days!

Bread was made from scratch. Lamb was roasted whole overnight on an outside spit, or at least its portions, in our oven. Yogurt was always made from good quality whole milk. Sweets were packed with nuts and dripped with honey. Nearly every portion of the vine was incorporated into food and wine. Dates, figs, apricots, olives, and rich sheep and goat's milk cheeses would grace the table while the cooking was still under way. The end of the meal was always accompanied by a shot of Arak and a thimble sized cup of black coffee.

This is the rich heritage that made me who I am, and I am proud to embrace all that is important to my sisters, our children and their little families. Once family, always family. Laugh if you must, or send your favorite shrink our way, but I tell you the truth, when people come into our family, sit at our table, share in the richness of our diverse eccentricities, they always return. Maybe it's that Genie lamp…

Spanakopita

SPANAKOPITA

Greece

"You do you, and I do me," said every Greek, Syrian, and Lebanese when it comes to boasting about the way they prepare spinach pies. The Middle Eastern style of preparing Fataya, (savory pies) is with bread dough, while the Greeks use phyllo. Both are delicious, and both can be time consuming.

So, I wanted to create all the flavors that go into these yummy, healthy pies, but not spend the time. Frozen tart shells were the perfect solution! These tart shells are made out of phyllo dough, and only need to be filled and baked. What a time saver!

Makes 24 Small Tarts

- Spinach – 1 lb. wilted in steam, drained, and pureed
- Onion – ½ cup, chopped small, sautéed in olive oil
- Olive oil – 1 tablespoon to saute onions
- Lemon – 2 tablespoons juice, 1 teaspoon zest
- Garlic – 1 clove, pressed
- Eggs – 2
- Oregano – 1 teaspoon dried or 1 tablespoon freshly chopped
- Feta – ½ inch square cubes, for each tart
- Tart shells – 24

Instruction

Mix pureed wilted spinach, sautéed onions, garlic, oregano, lemon juice/zest, and eggs together. Place a dollop of filling into tart shells. Place feta cubes on top of each filled tart shell. Place tarts on parchment lined cookie sheet.

Bake – 325 – Until tart shells are golden in color and the filling is firm to the touch. About 15 minutes.

KIBBEH

Syria & Lebanon

Nearly every country in the world has some type of a meatball. That being said… these are the best! (Okay Italians, I here you sneering!) Ground lamb, bulgur wheat, cinnamon, (yes, cinnamon!) stuffed with toasted pine nuts. Yum!

Growing up, we always baked them. In Brazil, influenced by a very large Lebanese population, they were fried. Fried Kibbeh in Brazil, stuffed with cheese, is very, very popular. In fact, kibbeh was so popular in Brazil that the grocery stores sold the wheat labeled just for Kibbeh, 'Kiepe-Ble.'

The secret to kibbeh that makes it different from most other meatballs, is its texture. Once the wheat has soaked, drained, puffed up, and has been added to the meat, it is kneaded, much like bread. Kneading the meat and grain together pulverizes the fat and amalgamates the separate ingredients into one.

Once balls are formed, large or tiny, a thumb (or pinky, if it is tiny balls) goes into the ball to make room for the stuffing, or not. Kibbeh is just fine without stuffing, but if you really want to wow a guest, simply saute onions and pine nuts in olive oil and herbs and spoon a little inside the meatball.

Kibbeh is always eaten with Lebne (thick yogurt). It is believed that yogurt aids in the digestion of meats, and wards off bacteria, particularly when meat is eaten raw.

My sisters and I grew up making Kibbeh with our mama when we were big enough to stand on a chair and take our little fists to the meat to knead. As they say, "All You Knead Is Love"!

Makes 2 dozen balls

- Ground lamb – 2 pounds
- Bulgur wheat – 1 ½ cups (also called cracked wheat)
- Cinnamon – 1 tablespoon
- Salt – 1 tablespoon (for kibbeh)
- Marjoram or Oregano – 1 tablespoon
- Lemon juice – 1 whole lemon
- Garlic – 2 cloves, crushed
- Salt – 1 ½ teaspoon (for wheat)
- Water – enough to cover the wheat

Instruction

Place the wheat, lemon juice, crushed garlic, and 11/2 teaspoons salt into a bowl and cover with water. Cover and let set overnight.

Place the lamb into a bowl and break up the meat. Squeeze all the liquid out of the wheat and add to the meat. Slowly begin to squeeze and knead the meat and wheat together, adding a little of the spices as you go, until all the spices are incorporated, and you can barely see the difference between the wheat and the meat. Roll into little footballs. Press your thumb down the center to make room for the stuffing.

Filling

- Onion – 1 large onion minced into tiny bits
- Pine nuts – 8 ounces
- Cinnamon – 1 teaspoon
- Salt – ½ teaspoon
- Butter – 4 ounces

Instruction

Melt butter. Add onions and cook on medium covered until soft. Add pine nuts and spices. Stir and cook open until the nuts begin to take a little bit of color. Turn off and let cool.

Place a small spoon (1/2 teaspoon size) into each cavity of lamb balls. Squeeze the open hole closed.

Preheat Oven 350

Place in a baking pan/dish and bake for 25 to 40 minutes, depending on the size of your kibbeh balls. You want the outer color to begin to brown but not over cooked.

Serve with thick yogurt or my Tzatziki recipe

Kibbeh

GRAPE LEAVES

Flying into Santa Rosa to film a Food Network show, took me back to a time when I was a little girl. It seemed we always had friends that had a vine or two in their back yard. When September rolled around, we were invited to come help harvest the leaves.

The work began. Several large stainless-steel pots would go onto the stove with water and a handful of salt and the leaves would be blanched, cooled, drained in readiness for stuffing. Stuffing was usually ground lamb and rice, but barley and lentils were also a favorite of ours. We did this for several days, with the help and fun of several other friends of my mom. In the end, everyone walked away with bundles of delicious stuffed grape leaves to tuck away in their freezer.

As my plane landed in Santa Rosa, the patchwork topography of the vineyards inspired me to compose a food reality story, smack dab in the middle of one of these vineyards, and later collaborate with some 'who's who' to produce it.

I got caught up in the excitement of the event as it began to unfold in my mind. Three 10-foot wooden farm tables with an assortment of eclectic chairs would be set into place in the harvested vineyard. The guests to dine would be an eclectic artsy bunch. Each guest would be asked to bring their own table place setting; cloth mat, napkin, dish, bowl, tableware, and glasses. For sure, each guest would seek not be outdone, and so the table would come together like no other carefully planned table setting. How whimsical, I thought.

The menu, well that had clearly begun to flash through my mind's eye. Each course would celebrate an aspect of the vineyard, from the wines, right down to the champagne sorbet served for dessert.

The menu:

- Long charcuterie boards set out featuring clusters of smoked chili batter tempura grapes, paired with beet blinis topped with a tiny dollop of mascarpone, tiny champagne grapes and a drizzle of balsamic reduction.

- Stuffed grape leaves, prepared Iranian style with rice, roasted garlic, raisins and nuts, rather than the meat and rice stuffing I grew up with.

- Large wooden troughs placed strategically down the center of the tables with fresh garden herbs, greens, drunken goat cheese, pistachios, grapes and strips of smoked turkey breast and dusted with crushed freeze-dried grapes.

- Small tabletop hibachis would be placed among the guests, prepared with dried vine twigs ready to be lit to roast lamb tenderloin strips, that have been marinated in port, honey, garlic and a pinch of ghost chili, and then carefully skewed onto freshly cut green vines twigs, so as not to burn.

- Loaves of fire roasted artisan breads abound, as does the lively conversation

- Trays of champagne sorbet, raisin-almond biscotti, and shots of Pernod to bring the dining to its finale.

And then my plane landed. I was quickly awakened from my dreamy premonition, whisked off to the studio where I never saw the light of day, nor one single grape. But I plan to revisit the lovely Santa Rosa vineyards again, and perhaps the perfect 'who's who' will appear to bring this lovely vineyard dining experience to life on film, for all the world to experience!

DOLMAS - STUFFED GRAPE LEAVES

Syria

Makes about 50

- Grape leaves – 16 oz. Jar, rinsed and drained (about 50)
- Rice – 1 cup, rinsed in water
- Ground lamb or beef – 1 pound
- Lemon juice – 1 lemon and zest
- Onion – 1 medium, chopped finely and sauteed in olive oil
- Olive oil – 2 teaspoons to saute onions
- Salt – ½ teaspoon

Instruction

Combine meat, rice, sautéed onions, and salt. Mix well.

Place one teaspoon of filling at the stem edge of the grape leaf and roll it up like a cigar. Layer the rolled grape leaves in a pot, one layer at a time, pressing each layer down gently. Once all leaves are wrapped, place a dish on top of the layers in the pot.

Add enough water to the pot to come just level with the dish. Cover pan and cook on low for 35 minutes until tender. During last 10 minutes of cooking, add lemon juice and zest. Any leftover filling can be frozen for another time.

Serve with yogurt.

Stuffed Grape Leaves

Stuffed Grape Leaves With Tzatziki

Beet Hummus

BEET HUMMUS

Syria - California

Having grown up with a bowl of hummus always available in our refrigerator, I thought everyone else did too. For us, it was kind of like peanut butter. We put it on crackers, smeared it on bread, dipped fresh veggies and chips into it, and it was healthy too!

Then, I grew up and suddenly everyone else was enjoying hummus because grocery stores across America caught on to this nutritionally rich, crazy delicious snack food, that fast began to stray from the original recipe. So, I strayed too!

With the influence from my Cali-kids, the traditional taste buds of my family, and my desire for something a little more colorful on the table, I created Beet Hummus. It is so darn delicious that I rarely make the beige colored hummus I grew up with.

- Chickpeas – 16 oz can, drained
- Beet root – golf ball size, peeled and cooked
- Tahini – 2 tablespoons
- Garlic – 2 cloves
- Lemon juice – 2 tablespoons
- Olive oil - 1 tablespoon, plus more to drizzle on top
- Salt – to taste

Instruction

In a blender or food processor, place all ingredients and puree until smooth. Taste for more salt or lemon, as you prefer. Serve on a low flat dish with a drizzle of olive oil on top and a sprinkle of freshly chopped herbs.

THE MENU

P&J BUTTONS

BABY BANANA BITES

PIZZA ON A STICK

GRANDMA'S SNEAKY MEATBALLS

SMALL PEEPS PLATES

The sweetest moments in my life, are when my grandchildren remind me of all the tender moments of when my children were little. Children bring out the child in me. My children loved to cook, even if they were pretending their blocks were pieces of food. Now my grandchildren cook, and it is usually with the real stuff!

These P&J Bites are a cookie dough pressed with a button, so they can be filled with anything kids like on a cookie or cracker. Mini muffin tins are a whimsical way to offer children a one-bite delight made from any favorite muffin recipe, sweet or savory, all of which Grandma will serve with tea. And yes, when the little cousins get together, the boys do stuff the girls like, and the girls do stuff the boys like, and that way, everyone is happy because there is always FOOD!

BABY BANANA BITES

Makes 4 Dozen mini muffins
- Bananas – 2 very ripe
- Eggs – 2
- Sugar – ½ cup
- Oil – ½ cup
- Yogurt – ½ cup

- Flour – 1 ½ cups
- Barley Flour or Oat flour – ½ cup
- Cardamom – 2 teaspoons (or ginger)
- Baking Powder – 2 teaspoons
- Baking Soda – ½ teaspoon
- Salt – ½ teaspoon

Instruction

Mix the wet ingredients well.

Emma

Instruction

Mix the dry ingredients into the wet. Place batter in mini paper lined muffin tins.

Bake at 350 until toothpick comes out clean. About 15 minutes.

Rebecca

Baby Banana Bites

Pizza Sticks

GRANDMA'S SNEAKY MEATBALLS

What little person doesn't love spaghetti, meatballs, and pizza!

Truth be known, I'm a tricky Grandma. I sneak green things in meatballs and tomato sauce. Shhh. I give the little one's veggies to cut up and don't tell them what it's for. When they aren't looking, I puree them in the processor and toss it into the meat or sauce. alakazam! Veggies disappear!

A fun way to serve the kids their favorite 'Grandma's Sneaky Meatballs' is on a stick. I simply make tiny bite-size meatballs, cook them, and then stack them on a stick with mozzarella, half a cherry tomato, and pizza dough pressed into tiny rounds, sprinkled with cheese and bake for 10 minutes. How fun is this!

Makes 12-24 (quarter size)

- Ground meat – 1 pound
- Egg – 1
- Grated Cheese – ¼ cup
- Bread crumbs – ¼ cup
- Ketchup – 1 tablespoon
- Salt & Pepper to taste
- Pureed veggies – 1 cup, anything you want (zucchini, kale, spinach, etc.)

Instruction

Mix it well. Make quarter size balls. Place on parchment paper and bake until brown on the outside, about 20 minutes. Use on pizza sticks or eat as they are.

Charles *David*

107

ALWAYS ROOM
THE SWEETEST WORDS

Most of the desserts I have come to know and love, are made from nuts, fruits, honey, and healthy raw ingredients. When I am serving a spread of small plates, I want my desserts to be in keeping with the visuals of the other plates I serve. These are a few of my favorite desserts, that are almost always in my kitchen!

THE MENU

LEMON BITES

PIE CRUST – MASON JAR LIDS

STRAWBERRY TARTS

BLACKBERRY VEGAN CHEESECAKE

BAKLAWA

CHOCOLATE DONUTS –
the counterfeit cook

CHOCOLATE DATES

LEMON BITES

Makes 8 small tarts

- Eggs – 2 whole plus 2 yolks
- Sugar – 1 cup
- Butter – 6 tablespoons, melted and cooled
- Lemon juice – 1 cup
- Corn starch – 1 tablespoon
- Salt – ½ teaspoon

Instruction

Whip the eggs and sugar until ribbons fall off the spoon.

Add melted butter and mix well.

Sprinkle corn starch across the lemon juice and give a whisk.

Add to the batter along with salt. Mix well.

Pour into prepared pie crust, store bought or *my* favorite.

Bake at 325 for 20 plus minutes, or until custard is firm. Serve as is, with a dollop of whipped cream or berries.

PIE CRUST – MASON JAR LIDS

Using the lids of these canning jars is simply a brilliant way to make petite desserts or savory pies. Simply invert the detachable lid, and you have an inexpensive tart pan. When the cooking is done, the crust pops out easily because the lid pops out too!

Makes 12

- Butter – 1 cold stick, cut up
- Flour – 1 ½ cups
- Sugar – 2 tablespoons
- Salt – ½ teaspoon
- Egg – 1
- Cold water – 2-4 tablespoons

Instruction

Place all ingredients into a food processor and blend until it forms a ball. Add a pinch of water or flour as need be. Roll out on a floured surface and prepare in lids.

STRAWBERRY TARTS

Strawberries, Raspberries, Fresh Figs, or any fruit of your liking, make for a delicious addition to the Lemon Bites, lemony custard tarts!

BLACKBERRY VEGAN CHEESECAKE

Makes 12 small pies (using mason jar lids)

Crust

- Pitted dates – 2 cups
- Raw cashews – 2 cups
- Cacao powder – 2 tablespoons
- Blend in a food processor. Make 12 balls and press into the bottom of tart lids. Chill.

Sweet Avocado Puree

- Avocado – 1 cut into chunks
- Cashew, Coconut, or Almond milk – ¾ cup
- Sugar – ½ cup, or stevia to taste
- Raw cashews – 1 cup, soaked for 30 minutes in water, and drained
- Powdered gelatin – 2 teaspoons, dissolved in 1 tablespoon water
- Lemon juice and zest – ½ lemon
- Matcha green tea powder – 1 tablespoon
- Puree all ingredients. Set a little aside to use as a dollop on top. Pour puree half way up chilled crust. Chill.

Blackberry Gelatin

- Blackberries – 2 cups, save a few for garnish
- Sugar – ½ cup, or stevia to taste
- Powdered gelatin – 1 tablespoon dissolved in 2 tablespoons water
- Violette or Blackberry Liqueur – 1 shot (optional)
- Full fat coconut milk – 13 oz. can

Instruction

Puree all ingredients. Pour evenly onto of the avocado puree. Chill for at least an hour or more until sets.

Pop out the bottom of the mason jar lid and slide the cheesecake onto a small dish. Spoon a tiny dollop of reserved avocado puree onto, and half a slice of blackberry.

BAKLAWA

Servings: 2 rolls with 8 – 10 slices per roll

Filling Ingredients

- Pistachios or your favorite nut – 4 cups
- Sugar – ½ cup
- Cinnamon – 1 tablespoon
- Egg - 1
- Salt – 1 teaspoon

Instruction

Place nuts, sugar, and spices in a food processor, (or blender) and blend until finely ground. Whisk egg, then pour into processor while running until ingredients for a paste. Set aside.

Syrup Ingredients

- Sugar – 1 cup
- Water or orange juice – ¾ cup
- Honey – ½ cup (agave, date, or coconut syrup can be used)
- Orange Blossom Water – 1 teaspoon (or vanilla)
- Place syrup ingredients in a saucepan, bring to a boil, lower, and simmer for about 15 minutes.
- Phyllo sheets – 8 sheets, using 4 sheets per roll
- Butter – 4 ounces, melted
- Orange rind – optional for finishing

Instruction

Preheat oven to 350. Place parchment paper on a baking sheet. Baste melted butter across the top of a phyllo sheet. Continue stacking one sheet at a time and baste, until you have four sheets basted. Place half of the prepared filling at the long end of the prepared phyllo stack. Fold the end over the filling, and roll the filling inside the dough, basting just a little melted butter as you roll.

Place on prepared baking sheet, seam side down. With a sharp knife, gently slice angled slices, (about an inch wide) just across the top of the roll, (this makes final slicing so much easier). Bake for about 25 – 35 minutes, until the tops are golden. Remove from the oven. Press a sharp knife, the remainder of the way through each slice, while pastry is hot/warm. Drizzle syrup across the slices, taking care to allow the syrup to seep into the slices. It is not necessary to use all the syrup, only enough to gently sweeten. Grate a little orange peel across the tops.

Baklawa

A PAGE AND A RECIPE FROM THE COUNTERFEIT COOK.

....

My sweet-tooth, oldest son Tomio, shares a favorite recipe with his mama, and you!

Tomio says:

"I was the kid on the school bus with the weird smelling lunch box. Growing up my mom wouldn't let us eat processed foods, so our lunch boxes were filled with things like hummus and other things no one in school would trade their lunch for. Fast forward to twenty-something years later and I am still eating the same stinky food, but this time by choice.

When I would go home to visit my mom, I started to realize the effects that eating crap food had on people I knew growing up. I live in SoCal now, so it is easier to stick to a way of eating that is healthy.

My biggest problem is that I LOVE sweets. Yea, salty foods are good and all, but sweets are where it's at. I have accumulated a massive collection of recipes over the years, and I decided to share them with you guys."

~The Counterfeit Cook~

CHOCOLATE DONUTS

Mmm, doooonutsss! There isn't much I can say about these donuts, except that you HAVE to try them. Seriously, stop reading this and go preheat your oven.

Makes 12

Cake

- Almond flour – 1 cup
- Agave or Honey – 4 tablespoons
- Eggs – 2, large
- Cocoa powder – 1 tablespoon
- Baking soda – ¼ teaspoon

Icing

- Powdered sugar – ¾ cup
- Cocoa powder – 3 tablespoons
- Almond milk – 2-3 tablespoons
- Vanilla extract – ½ teaspoon
- Rainbow sprinkles – ¼ cup

Instruction

Preheat oven to 325

Grease your donut pan and set aside. In a medium mixing bowl, mix together all the cake ingredients until smooth. Fill donut pan with mixture ½ way full.

Bake for 10 – 15 minutes, keeping an eye on them. Donuts are cooked when a toothpick inserted comes out clean. Cool on a wire rack and mix icing. Dip each donut into the chocolate icing and sprinkle with a little of the rainbow sprinkles.

Healthy with a twist of naughty

CHOCOLATE DATES

Makes 3 dozen

- Dates – 2 cups, pitted
- Nuts – 2 cups, your favorite
- Cacao – 2 tablespoons
- Chocolate for dipping – 1 cup melted
- Coconut flakes, or crushed nuts – for final coating

Instruction

Puree dates, nuts, and cacao in a processor until it forms a paste. Using a melon-ball scooper or small spoon, make round balls. Using a toothpick or fork, dip in melted chocolate and roll in coconut or crushed nuts. Place on parchment paper, and pop into the fridge to chill a bit. These are truly my favorite dessert!

CLOSING

IN CLOSING this fun excursion with you, I hope I have encouraged you in some small meaningful way to rethink your plates.

Plates… Speaking of plates, I want to leave you with this thought, "The family that cooks together stays together, but the family that teaches their little ones to wash the dishes, will pass on some of the most fun-loving memories of conversation and laughter, right there over that kitchen sink!" Oh, how I remember the stories, the gossip, the laughter, the problems solved, that took place over a kitchen sink!

William

RECIPE INDEX